Take a Stand! Medieval Civilizations

Socratic Discussion in History

Student's Edition

Copyright ©2019 by The Classical Historian. All Rights Reserved

DEDICATION

Dedicated to Zdenka and the De Gree Kids

Copyright © 2019 by John De Gree. All rights reserved
Painting by Fran Johnston, Used with permission, © 2019 by John De Gree. All rights reserved.
Edited by Jessica De Gree
Published by The Classical Historian, San Clemente, California 92673.

No part of this work may be reproduced or transmitted in any form or by any means, electronic or mechanical, including photocopying and recording, or by any information storage or retrieval system without the prior written permission of the publisher. Address inquiries to www.classicalhistorian.com

Copyright ©2019 by The Classical Historian. All Rights Reserved

Table of Contents

Week One: Geography of Arabia and the beginning of Islam___1

Week Two: The Spread of Islam: The Caliphs___5

Week Three: Medieval Islamic Science, Math, Business, Literature, Art, and

    Architecture___8

Week Four: The Decline of the Islamic Empire and The Seljuk and Ottoman Turks_11

Week Five: Growth of Islam in the Medieval Ages___15

Week Six: Sui, Tang, and Song Dynasties___18

Week Seven: Medieval China___19

Week Eight: Mongols and the Ming Dynasty___23

Week Nine: Medieval Japan___24

Week Ten: Medieval India___27

Week Eleven: Medieval Korea and Medieval Southeast Asia___28

Week Twelve: Geography of Africa___29

Week Thirteen: Medieval West African Empires and Economy,

    Medieval East Africa and Zimbabwe___30

Week Fourteen: Medieval Eastern Roman (Byzantine) Empire___34

Week Fifteen: Geography of Europe, Barbarian Empire___35

Week Sixteen: Spread of Christianity and Roman Values into Barbarian Europe___36

Week Seventeen: Founding of Western Europe, Founding of England and Ireland___37

Week Eighteen: Feudalism ___38

Week Nineteen: The Age of Faith, Medieval Art and Education ___39

Week Twenty: The Crusades, Conflict between Kings and Popes ___40

Week Twenty-One: Medieval Europe ___41

Week Twenty-Two: Liberty, Muslims, and Jews ___46

Week Twenty-Three: The Fall of Medieval Society ___47

Week Twenty-Four: The Renaissance

    Grammar ___48

    Reading ___49

Week Twenty-Five: The Reformation

    Grammar ___55

    Reading ___56

Week Twenty-Six: The Scientific Revolution

    Grammar ___63

    Reading ___65

Week Twenty-Seven: The Age of Exploration

    Grammar ___70

    Reading ___71

Week Twenty-Eight: Great Civilizations of Mesoamerica and South America_____76

Week Twenty-Nine: The Mayas and the Incas_____77

Week Thirty: Incas and Northeast Tribes_____78

Week Thirty-One: Southeast, Plains, Great Basin, and Plateau Indians_____79

Week Thirty-Two: Southwest, California, Northwest Coastal, Subarctic,

and Arctic Tribes_____80

Grammar Week One
Geography of Arabia and The Beginnings of Islam

1. What is Arabia?   It is a peninsula.

2. What is a peninsula?   It is a body of land surrounded by water on three sides.

3. Who were Bedouins?   Bedouins were nomads who were fierce warriors.

4. What are oases?   Oases are natural springs in Arabia.

5. What do you find near large oases?   Near large oases you find cities.

6. When was Muhammad born?   570

7. What religion did Muhammad found and what do we call its believers?   He founded Islam and believers are called Muslims.

8. How many wives did Muhammad have?   11

9. How many wives can Muslims have?   4

10. What is the holy book of Islam?   The Koran

11. List two of the five pillars of Islam:
a. Pray five times a day
b. Give to the community

12. What is the name of the building Muslims worship in?   Muslims worship God in a mosque.

Fact or Opinion?

Fact

A **fact** in history is a statement that is accepted as true and is not debatable. A fact often refers to a date, a person, or a document. For example, "The Declaration of Independence was written and signed in 1776." We know this happened because we have the original document, the men who wrote and signed this document wrote about it, and observers wrote about it as well. There is no doubt in anybody's mind whether the facts in this statement are true.

Which of these sentences are facts and which are not?

Fact or Not a Fact?		
__	1.	The first Egyptian settlements were near the Euphrates River.
__	2.	Early civilizations often settled near major rivers.
__	3.	Another way of saying Old Stone Age is Paleolithic.
__	4.	Early man used guns to hunt buffaloes.
__	5.	California has the best waves to surf in the United States.

Opinion

An **opinion** is an expression of somebody's ideas and is debatable. Opinions that are based on facts and good reasoning are stronger than opinions not based on facts. In history, opinions alone tend to be less persuasive than when a person supports his opinions with facts.

Are the following opinions or facts?

Opinion or Fact?		
__	1.	Life for early man was more peaceful than our life today.
__	2.	Teachers who are nice don't assign homework.
__	3.	Almost everybody's favorite food is pizza.
__	4.	Mesopotamia means "the land between two rivers."
__	5.	Sumerians were the first people to use wheeled vehicles.

Now that you've learned the difference between fact and opinion, read the example paragraphs below and answer the questions. These two students attempted to answer the question "Did the ancient civilizations of Mesopotamia contribute much to world civilizations?"

Student 1: The ancient civilizations of Mesopotamia contributed much to the world. These societies rocked! When there was a really big war, the Sumerians and Assyrians knew how to fight hard. These societies would use a lot of arrows in their battles, and the enemy wouldn't know how to respond. Most of the time, the enemy would just die, or quit. Also, everyone knows that Mesopotamia had the best kind of clothing. Have you seen pictures of the great Babylonian kings? Their clothing was "tight." And, Mesopotamia was the land between two rivers, so therefore this area had to have a lot of water. All in all, the ancient civilizations of Mesopotamia contributed much to the world.

Student 2: The ancient civilizations of Mesopotamia contributed much to the world. The Sumerians created the first written language. We call this "Cuneiform." Sumerians also were the first people to use the wheel for transportation. The Babylonian king Hammurabi established one of the first written law codes, known as Hammurabi's Code. These laws helped the weak against the strong, protected women's property rights, and regulated doctors' fees. Also, the Hittites discovered how to use iron, which at that time was the strongest metal in the world that humans could work with. Phoenicians gave us the world's first alphabet, with 22 symbols. In addition, the Hebrews were the first people ever to worship only one God. Yes, the ancient civilizations of Mesopotamia contributed much to the world.

Questions

1. Which of these two students uses more opinion than fact? _____

2. Copy one sentence that is an opinion. _____

3. Copy one sentence that details at least one fact. _____

4. Which of these two students' writings is more persuasive? Why? _____

Judgment

Judgment in social studies means a person's evaluation of facts. For example, if we use the fact that the Romans believed citizens could vote, we can judge from this that the Romans looked somewhat favorably on democracy. Good judgment is very persuasive but bad judgment is not.

Write facts and judgments in the spaces provided. Discuss your judgments in class.

Fact:	11-year-old Maria Perez won the gold medal in the city 800-meter sprint.
Judgment:	Maria is a fast runner.

Fact:	Private Smith was killed in war and had one wife and 7 children.
Judgment:	Private Smith's death was a tragedy.

Fact:	Thursday's temperature in Santa Ana was 105 degrees Fahrenheit.
Judgment:	Thursday was very hot.

Make your own.

Fact:
Judgment:

Fact:
Judgment:

Fact:
Judgment:

Grammar for Week Two
The Spread of Islam: The Caliphs

1. What is the successor of Muhammad called?   Caliph

2. Who is a Shiite? He is a Muslim who thinks the Caliph should be a blood relative of Muhammad.

3. Who is a Sunni?   He is a Muslim who thinks the Caliph doesn't have to be a blood relative of Muhammad.

4. What did Muslim armies do from about 600 – 1100? They conquered many territories and converted many people to Islam.

5. What is jihad? It is a Holy War for Muslims.

6. Who invaded Spain and tried to conquer Europe?   Muslims

7. Who conquered the Christian Holy Land from the Romans? Muslims

Supporting Evidence

Supporting evidence refers to everything you use to support your thesis. These include, but are not limited to, the following.

1. Diaries and journals
2. Government documents such as birth certificates
3. Songs and stories
4. Coins, medals, jewelry
5. Artistic works such as pictures and paintings
6. Tools and pottery
7. Documents such as the Declaration of Independence
8. Weapons
9. Burial remains
10. Literature and customs

Good writers overwhelm the reader with so many pieces of supporting evidence that the writing will be quickly accepted. Also, the writer has a duty to explain carefully and logically the meaning of the evidence, showing how it supports the thesis. A writer must be careful, however, not to include unnecessary evidence. For example, the fact that Lincoln was born in a log cabin isn't evidence that he was a good president. Also, the dates a president was born and died may be evidence, but they would not support a thesis arguing who was the best president.

Practice

With your teacher discuss which of the following is evidence for the topic "Explain what daily life was like in the Roman Republic in the third century B.C."
1. A diary from 234 B.C: _____
2. A newspaper article from A.D. 250: _____
3. Your friend likes the subject: _____
4. A movie about life in the third century B.C: _____
5. A song Romans sang in the third century B.C: _____
6. A story on the crucifixion of Christ: _____
7. A painting of a Roman slave working in 299 A.D: _____

Primary or Secondary Source Analysis

A **primary source** is a piece of evidence authored by a person who witnessed or experienced a historical event. For example, diaries and journals are primary sources. It is usually better to find out something from a person who experienced a particular event than to hear about it secondhand. Primary source documents are usually the most useful for historians.

A **secondary source** is a piece of evidence that has been worked on by somebody who was not a witness to the historical event. Examples of secondary sources are textbooks, documentaries, and encyclopedias. Secondary sources are valuable but not as valuable as primary sources. Secondary sources contain the bias of the writer. This means that the writer of a secondary source will put his ideas into his explanation of the historical event, even when he may be trying not to.

Take a look at these two examples regarding the same event.
Event: Car accident outside of school

Example 1: "Oh no! I was in the back seat of my mom's car. This kid threw his friend's handball onto the street. All of a sudden, his friend jumped in front of my mom's car to get his ball. He didn't even look if a car was coming. My mom hit him and his body smashed against our windshield. Blood was everywhere!"

Example 2: "Did you hear what happened? Mario told me that his brother was walking home when he dropped his handball onto the street. After his brother looked both ways for cars, he stepped out onto the street to get his ball. Then this mad lady came speeding down the street and aimed her car at him. She hit him on purpose!"

Questions
1. Which is a primary source?
2. Which is a secondary source?
3. What is usually more believable, a primary or secondary source? Why?

Grammar for Week Three
Medieval Islamic Science, Math, Business, and Literature;
Medieval Islamic Art and Architecture

1. When was the Islamic Golden Age?   About 700s to 1200s

2. To make money what did many Muslims do?   They traded gold, salt, copper, and slaves in markets around the world.

3. What did Avicenna write?   He wrote one of the world's first encyclopedias.

4. Why were Muslims not able to depict humans in art?   Muslims were afraid people would worship the artwork.

5. What is arabesque?   Arabesque is a design that resembles flowers or vines.

6. What is the Taj Mahal?   It is a Muslim mausoleum.

7. Name one major Islamic city where much trading occurred. Meccah

8. What do Muslims consider as the holiest site? Mosque of the Prophet in Medina

Using Quotes

A **quote** is when a writer uses the exact words of another writer. An effective analytical essay in social studies will use quotes. For example, an essay about the use of violence in the Middle Ages will be stronger if certain quotes from this time period are used. When you argue a point about the past, there is no better evidence than a primary source document or quote.

Look at the example below. The paragraph is part of an answer to the question "Was the plague a problem in ancient Greece?"

The plague was most certainly a problem to the ancient Greeks. The Greek historian Thucydides, in "The Peloponnesian Wars," wrote, "Words indeed fail one when one tries to give a general picture of this disease; and as for the sufferings of individuals, they seemed almost beyond the capacity of human nature to endure." To the ancient Greeks, the plague was a serious problem.

When using quotes, write the original author's name and the speech or document from which the quote was taken from. Punctuate correctly with quotation marks.

Practice

Practice writing three quotations taken from your textbook. Use correct punctuation! Pay attention to the commas, the quotation marks, and the end marks. For example, Julius Caesar, when crossing the Rubicon River, said, "The die is cast."

1. _____

2. _____

3. _____

Paraphrasing

Paraphrasing means to take information from your research and to put it in your own words. This is an important skill to have when writing a research paper. If you copy directly from a source, such as a book, but do not place the words in quotation marks and write the author's name, it is called **plagiarism**. Plagiarism is against the rules of writing and your teacher will not accept the work!

Here is an example of paraphrasing a quote from a teacher.

Quote:
"China's mountainous geography made it very difficult for Chinese leaders to unify their country."
Paraphrase:
Ancient Chinese leaders had a hard time unifying their country because of the many mountains in China.

Practice

Quote:
"Confucius lived in a time of turmoil in China. He wrote about respecting parents and authority. Many Chinese grew to believe in what Confucius wrote about."
Paraphrase:
_____
_____
_____

Quote:
"The Chinese were great traders with other cultures. The Silk Road ran from China through central Asia to the Middle East. Along this trail, Chinese met with Arabs, Africans, Europeans, and other Asians."
Paraphrase:
_____
_____
_____
_____

Grammar for Week Four
The Decline of the Islamic Empire;
The Seljuk and Ottoman Turks

1. Who destroyed much of the Islamic Empires in the Medieval Ages? The Mongols destroyed the Islamic Empires in the Medieval Ages, and the Christian Crusaders made it weaker.
2. Who was Genghis Khan? He was the leader of the Mongols.
3. What was the purpose of the Crusades? Christians wanted to be able to visit the Holy Land and to win the Holy Land back from the Muslims.
4. What was the Reconquista? It was a 700-year war the Spanish Catholics fought against the Muslims in Spain. The Spanish won in 1492.
5. Who conquered most of the Arab Muslim Empire and then established a new Empire in the 11th century? The Turks did.
6. How did the Turks treat Christian pilgrims trying to visit the Holy Land?
7. The Turks abused the pilgrims and would not allow them to visit the Holy Land.
8. Why did Pope Urban II call for a Crusade against the Muslim Turks?
9. The Pope wanted Christians to visit the Holy Land and to win the Holy Land back from the Muslims.
10. What was the result of the Crusades? The Turks won, but the Christians won the right to visit the Holy Land.
11. Who were the Ottoman Turks? The Ottoman Turks were an Asian people who conquered Arab Muslim Empires. The Turks were pagans, but converted to Islam.
12. Who were the Janissary Corps? The Turks invaded Europe and stole young Christian boys. The Turks trained the boys to be vicious fighters and to be Muslims. The Janissary Corps was a fierce army made up of kidnapped Christian boys.
13. What happened to Constantinople? The Turks conquered it. The Christians fled to Europe. The Turks renamed it Istanbul.
14. What did the Sultan try to do to Europe? The Sultan tried to conquer Europe and make it Muslim.
15. What was the last battle that stopped the Sultan and the Turks from conquering Europe? The Battle of Lepanto.

Open-Ended Socratic History Question #1
Islamic Civilizations

In the seventh century A.D., one of the world's most important religions emerged on the Arabian Peninsula. Muhammad, a seventh-century Arab, began the religion of Islam, whose followers are called Muslims. Muslims call Muhammad the Prophet and they believe that there is one God, Allah. By Muhammad's death in A.D. 632, many of the people of Arabia were Muslim. In the next 120 years Muslims spread their religion through Asia, North Africa, and Spain.

Medieval Islamic civilizations contributed much to the world in the areas of science, geography, mathematics, philosophy, medicine, art, literature, and through trade. Based on your research, what were two of the greatest contributions Muslims made to world civilizations? Use your lessons from World History Detective and from the primary source documents to answer your question. You may use other sources, as well.

A. Medieval Islamic Contributions

Contribution	Description
1. The religion of Islam	1. A monotheistic religion
2.	2.
3.	3.
4.	4.
5.	5.

B. Importance of Contributions Today

How is this contribution important today?
1.
2.
3.
4.
5.

C. Rating of Contributions

Rating, in order of importance	Reason for rating
1.	1.
2.	2.
3.	3.
4.	4.
5.	5.

Socratic Discussion and Reflection

When you share ideas with other students, your ideas may be reinforced, rejected, or slightly changed. Listening to your classmates' ideas will help you form your own judgment. After the class discussion, write the answer to the following question, "Based on your research, what were two of the greatest contributions Muslims made to world civilizations?"

_____
_____
_____
_____
_____
_____
_____
_____
_____
_____
_____
_____
_____
_____
_____
_____
_____
_____
_____
_____
_____
_____
_____
_____

Week Five: Growth of Islam in Medieval Ages
Open-Ended Socratic History Discussion #2

In a very short span of time, Islam spread from the two desert towns of Mecca and Medina throughout all of Arabia, North Africa, Persia, and Southeastern Europe. In about 150 years, Islam became the dominant religion in an area that had been predominantly Christian, Jewish, and pagan.

Through researching your lessons in World History Detective, the primary sources found at The Classical Historian website, and any other sources, answer the question, "What was the primary reason for the quick spread of Islam from 622 to 750?"

A. Growth of Islamic Empire using Maps

1. On page 128 of *World History Detective*, the map depicts the Roman Empire around the year A.D. 425. At this time, the Roman Empire was Catholic Christianity. Describe the geographical area that was predominantly Christian based on the map. _____

2. On page 137 of *World History Detective*, the Byzantine Empire under Emperor Justinian in the year 576 is depicted. The religious belief of the Byzantine Empire was Catholic Christianity. Describe the geographical area that was predominantly Christian based on the map. _____

3. On page 205 of *World History Detective*, the spread of Islam is shown from 622 – 732. Describe the areas where Islam spread. _____

B. The Growth of Islam

Read lessons 49. The Beginnings of Islam and 50. The Spread of Islam: The Caliphs. From these two lessons, what were the reasons for the spread of Islam? _____

C. Quotes from the Koran

On this website, https://www.classicalhistorian.com/free-primary-sources.html , read "Quotes from the Koran" and answer the question. Write here what the Koran states about war and fighting: _____

D. Socratic Discussion and Reflection

When you share ideas with other students, your ideas may be reinforced, rejected, or slightly changed. Listening to your classmates' ideas will help you form your own judgment. After the class discussion, write the answer to the following question, "Based on your research, "What was the primary reason for the growth of Islam from 622 to 750?"

_____
_____
_____
_____
_____
_____
_____
_____
_____
_____
_____
_____
_____
_____
_____
_____
_____
_____
_____
_____
_____
_____

Grammar for Week Six
Sui, Tang, and Song Dynasties

1. Which continent is the largest in the world?   Asia

2. Which mountain range is the highest in the world?   Himalayas

3. Which mountain is the highest in the world?   Mt. Everest

4. In which continent did all of the world's most followed religions begin?   Asia

5. Which area in the world is the coldest?   Siberia

6. What did ancient Chinese call people from other nations?   Barbarians

7. Built in ancient times, what links two great rivers of China today?   The Grand Canal

8. Name two medieval Chinese dynasties?   Sui, Tang, or Song

9. What trade route linked Asia to the rest of the world?   The Silk Road

10. Under the Tang, how did a person get a government job?   He took a test.

11. What was invented under the Song Dynasty?   Gunpowder, paper, block printing, advanced navigational tools.

Open-Ended Socratic History Discussion #3
Medieval China

Medieval China was arguably the world's most advanced and strongest civilization. The first two great medieval Chinese dynasties, the Tang and the Sung, made China a leading civilization. The dynasties of Tang (A.D. 618–907) and Sung (A.D. 960–1279) are known for great agricultural, technological, medical, mathematical, academic, literary, and commercial developments. In time, Chinese inventions and techniques would spread throughout the world.

Research the greatest contributions that the Chinese made to world civilizations in the Tang and Sung period. Using this research, answer the question "What were the two most important Chinese contributions to world civilizations during the Tang and Sung dynasties?" Explain your choices in detail.

A. Tang Dynasty (A.D. 618–907)

Tang contribution	Describe what it was and how it was important
1.	1.
2.	2.
3.	3.
4.	4.
5.	5.

B. Sung Dynasty (A.D. 960–1279)

Sung contribution	Describe what it was and how it was important
1.	1.
2.	2.
3.	3.
4.	4.
5.	5.

C. Prioritize the Contributions
Place the contributions in order of importance to the world.

Contribution	Describe what it was and how it was important
1.	1.
2.	2.
3.	3.
4.	4.
5.	5.

D. The Words of Marco Polo

In 1295, Marco Polo returned to Venice after living and working in China for 25 years. Although he experienced China under a Mongol leader, Kublai Khan, Marco Polo witnessed the advanced society that the Tang and Sung dynasties had created. While in a jail cell in Genoa (a city in present-day Italy), he shared his experiences with Rustichello, a writer. Rustichello wrote the stories of Marco Polo, and these stories spread throughout Europe. Below is an account by Marco Polo of a city of China.

> "Inside the city there is a Lake which has a compass of some 30 miles and all round it are erected beautiful palaces and mansions, of the richest and most exquisite structure that you can imagine, belonging to the nobles of the city…In the middle of the Lake are two Islands, on each of which stands a rich, beautiful and spacious edifice, furnished in such style as to seem fit for the palace of an Emperor. And when any one of the citizens desired to hold a marriage feast, or to give any other entertainment, it used to be done at one of these palaces.

Polo, Marco, "The Glories of Kinsay [Hangchow] (c. 1300") , From The Book of Ser Marco Polo the Venetian concerning the Kingdoms and Marvels of the East, trans. and ed. by Henry Yule, 3rd ed. revised by Henri Cordier (London: John Murray, 1903), Vol II. Pp. 185-193, 200-205, 215-216,

Paraphrase

To the best of your ability, paraphrase the above quote:

E. Socratic Discussion and Reflection

When you share ideas with other students, your ideas may be reinforced, rejected, or slightly changed. Listening to your classmates' ideas will help you form your own judgment. After the class discussion, write the answer to the following question, "Based on your research, "What were the two most important Chinese contributions to world civilizations during the Tang and Sung dynasties?"

_____
_____
_____
_____
_____
_____
_____
_____
_____
_____
_____
_____
_____
_____
_____
_____
_____
_____
_____
_____
_____
_____
_____

Grammar for Week Eight
Mongols and the Ming Dynasty

1. Who lived as shepherds on the steppe of Northern China?   Mongols

2. Who organized these shepherds of Northern China to form the largest empire in the history of the world?   Genghis Khan

3. What is cavalry? Horse mounted soldiers

4. Which Mongol ruler was the grandson of Genghis Khan and the Emperor of China? Kublai Khan

5. Which European worked for Kublai Khan for many years? Marco Polo

6. Did the Chinese enjoy being ruled by the Mongols or did the Chinese hate being ruled by the Mongols? The Chinese hated the Mongols.

7. Which dynasty overthrew the Mongols? The Ming Dynasty

8. Under the Ming Dynasty, did China open or close itself to the world? China isolated itself to the world.

Grammar for Week Nine
Medieval Japan

1. What is a chain of islands?   Archipelago

2. What did the ancient Japanese believe about the sun? They believed that the sun first rose and first set over Japan.

3. What was the religion of medieval Japanese? Shinto. They believed in many gods. The second main religion was Buddhism.

4. Today's emperor can trace his family back to which medieval clan? The Yamato

5. What were Japanese military rulers called?   Shogun

6. What were the land-owning lords called in Japan?   Daimyo

7. What were the medieval warriors called? Samurai

8. What is the samurai honor code called? Bushido

9. Who were hired spies or assassins during medieval Japan? Ninjas

10. Who tried to conquer medieval Japan? Kublai Khan

11. What did the Japanese believe defeated Kublai Khan on the ocean? The Kamikazi - the wind of the gods.

Open-Ended Socratic History Discussion #4
Medieval Japan

Compare and contrast the Samurai and the Ninja warriors of Medieval Japan.

A. Samurai or Ninja

1. Who were the samurai? _____
_____
_____

2. What was the relationship of the samurai and the peasants? _____
_____
_____

3. What was Bushido? _____
_____
_____

4. What was seppuku? _____
_____

5. Who were the ninja? _____
_____

6. Name one way the ninja were different than the samurai? _____
_____
_____

7. Who would a medieval Japanese hire if he wanted someone to do something unethical, a samurai or a ninja? Why? _____
_____
_____
_____

B. Compare and Contrast
Write the similarities and differences of samurais and ninjas.

Samurai   **Ninja**

Differences   Similarities   Differences
_____
_____
_____
_____
_____
_____
_____
_____
_____
_____
_____

C. Socratic Discussion and Reflection
When you share ideas with other students, your ideas may be reinforced, rejected, or slightly changed. Listening to your classmates' ideas will help you form your own judgment. After the class discussion, write the answer to the following prompt, "Compare and Contrast the samurai with the ninja.

_____
_____
_____
_____
_____
_____
_____
_____
_____
_____
_____
_____

Grammar for Week Ten
Medieval India

1. Himalayas: The Himalayas is the world's largest mountain range and it is located in India.

2. Hinduism: Hinduism is the religion of the majority of Indians.

3. Reincarnation: Hindus believe that a person is reborn into another body.

4. Delhi Sultanate: In 1206, Turkish Muslims established an Islamic kingdom in Northern India and ruled until 1526.

5. Mughal Empire: In 1526, the Mongol Muhammad Babur established the Mughal Empire that ruled India for 200 years.

6. Taj Mahal: The Taj Mahal is a beautiful white marble mausoleum built in the Mughal Empire.

7. Portuguese in India: Beginning in 1498, Portuguese sailors traded with Indians and Portuguese Indian Catholic missionaries brought Christianity.

Grammar for Week Eleven
Medieval Korea and Medieval Southeast Asia

1. Korea: Korea is a peninsula that borders China and is 79 miles from Japan.

2. Silla Dynasty: The Silla Dynasty united nearly all of Korea in 735.

3. Koryo Dynasty: The Koryo Dynasty ruled Korea from 918-1392.

4. Joseon (Choson) Dynasty: The Choseon Dynasty ruled Korea from 1392 to 1910.

5. Invaders of Medieval Korea: The Mongols, Chinese, and Japanese invaded Korea and ruled Korea intermittently in the medieval ages.

6. IndoChina: Southeast Asia is also called IndoChina because of the strong Indian and Chinese influence on the region.

7. Religions of Medieval Southeast Asia: Hinduism, Buddhism, Confucianism, Islam

8. Nam Viet: Nam Viet was a medieval kingdom in Southeast Asia. For many centuries, China ruled Nam Viet.

9. Khmer Empire: The Khmer Empire was the most powerful medieval kingdom in Southeast Asia.

10. Angkor: Angkor was the capital of the medieval Khmer Empire.

Grammar for Week Twelve
Geography of Africa

1. Name the second largest continent. Africa

2. Why do we call Africa a plateau continent? Africa is a plateau continent because most of it is 3,000 feet above sea level.

3. Name the world's largest desert. Sahara

4. What provides excellent farmland in northern Egypt? The Nile River

5. What is the large river in West Africa? The Niger River

6. Name the main products of medieval Africa: gold, salt, copper, iron, and slaves

7. Why was medieval Africa isolated? The plateau and Sahara Desert made it difficult for outsiders to venture into Africa.

8. What enabled Europeans to explore Africa? Inventions like the compass, astrolabe, and better ships enabled Europeans to explore Africa.

Grammar for Week Thirteen
Medieval West African Empires and Economics;
Medieval East Africa and Zimbabwe

1. What challenge do historians have in learning about ancient and medieval Africa? Outside of Egypt, Africans had no written language.

2. What river in West Africa was the site of 3 great medieval civilizations? The Nile River

3. How did people of Ghana earn money? They traded gold, diamonds, and slaves.

4. If you were a West African woman, what wouldn't you like? Your husband could have as many wives as he could afford.

5. What did North African Muslims trade with Ghana? Salt, tools

6. Who was Mansa Musa? HE was a fabulously wealthy king of Ghana.
7. What were the Swahili city-states? These were small kingdoms on the east coast of Africa where the people did much trading with Asia.

8. What religion spread to East Africa in the 10th century? Islam

9. What was unique about the Zimbabwe king? Only his wives and court were allowed to see him.

10. How was Zimbabwe protected? Zimbabwe had a huge stone wall around the city.

11. Which country conquered the Swahili city-states in 1480? Portugal

Open-Ended Socratic History Question #5
Medieval Africa

The power of the medieval African empires of Ghana and Mali rested in part on the business of trading. Africans traded with Arabian Muslims gold, salt, food, slaves, copper, and weapons. Because of this trade, the Arabic language and the Islamic religion spread in Africa. Also, the African empires of Ghana and Mali were able to trade for needed products, such as salt. Ghana and Mali became two of the richest empires in Africa, and perhaps in the world.

One product the Africans traded to the Muslims was the slave. Usually prisoners of war or criminals were used as slaves. In modern society in the United States, we view slavery as an evil. In Africa and in much of the world in the medieval ages, though, it was seen as normal. Answer the question "What were the two most important reasons Africans traded Africans as slaves?"

A. Trading in Medieval Africa

Items Traded	
From Ghana and Mali to Arabia	**From Arabia to Ghana and Mali**
1.	1.
2.	2.
3.	3.
4.	4.
5.	5.

B. Islamic Influence in Africa

Because of the trans-Saharan caravan trading between Africa and Arabia, Africa adopted many religious and cultural characteristics of Arabia. List the ways how Islamic Arabia influenced and changed Africa.

1.
2.
3.
4.
5.

C. Questions

Questions

1. What did Ghana and Mali trade to Arabia?_____
2. What did Arabia trade to Ghana and Mali?_____
3. Did Ghana and Mali receive Arabian items needed for survival? If so, what item(s)?_
_____
4. Did medieval Africa benefit from the trans-Saharan trade? How or how not?_____
_____
5. What did Arabians and Africans think about slavery? Did they think buying and selling humans was wrong, right, normal, or abnormal?_____
_____

C. Socratic Discussion and Reflection

When you share ideas with other students, your ideas may be reinforced, rejected, or slightly changed. Listening to your classmates' ideas will help you form your own judgment. After the class discussion, write the answer to the following prompt, "What were the two most important reasons Africans traded Africans as slaves?"

_____
_____
_____
_____
_____
_____
_____
_____
_____
_____
_____
_____
_____
_____
_____
_____
_____
_____
_____
_____
_____
_____

Grammar for Week Fourteen
Medieval Eastern Roman (Byzantine) Empire

1. When did the Medieval Ages begin?   A.D. 476

2. What do some historians call the Eastern Roman Empire? The Byzantine Empire

3. Who named the city of Constantinople? Constantine

4. Between which two continents lies Constantinople?

5. In the 500s, which emperor defeated many barbarian tribes to expand the Eastern Roman Empire? Justinian

6. Which barbarian people conquered Spain? Visigoths

7. What year did the Eastern Roman Empire fall to the Muslim Turks? 1453

8. Who conquered the Holy Land from the Christians of the Eastern Roman Empire in the 600s? Arab Muslims

Grammar for Week Fifteen
Geography of Europe, Barbarian Europe

1. Which continent is the second smallest?   Europe

2. What mountains form the eastern border of Europe? Ural Mountains

3. What makes travelling in Europe easier? Rivers

4. What ocean is to the west of Europe? Atlantic Ocean

5. What mountains form the eastern border of Europe? Urals

6. What mountains separate Italy from the rest of Europe? Alps

7. What is the largest European mountain? Mount Blanc

8. What is unique about Europe and farming? Europe is the continent with the largest percentage of farmable land.

9. What is Europe's largest river? Volga

10. Does Europe have many natural resources? Yes

11. What is the study of a civilization before writing?   Prehistory

12. About when were the Medieval Ages?   476 A.D. – 1500

13. What did the Romans call the Germanic, Slavic, and Celtic tribes who had no written language? Barbarians

14. Which people of Asia conquered large areas of land in the fourth the fifth centuries? The Huns

15. Which Germanic tribe established the country of France?   The Franks

16. Which tribes established the country of England?   Angles, Saxons, and Jutes

17. In 51 B.C., which people practiced human sacrifices? The Germanic barbarians

18. How did early Germanic tribes determine if someone were innocent or guilty? Trial by ordeal

19. What did the Germanic, Slavic, and Celtic peoples believe in? They believed in many gods. They were pagans.

20. What played a prominent role in the European pagan religions? Nature

Grammar for Week Sixteen
The Spread of Christianity and Roman Values into Barbarian Europe

1. What was one institution that survived the collapse of the Roman Empire? The Roman Catholic Church

2. Who was the leader of the Roman Catholic Church? The pope

3. What religious belief were the Catholics? Christians

4. Who converted the European barbarians of the middle ages to Christianity? The monks, nuns, and Catholics

5. Who was the missionary to the Irish? St. Patrick

6. Who was the missionary to the Germans? St. Boniface

7. Who was the missionary to the English? St. Augustine of Canterbury

8. Who established the first monastery? St. Benedict

Grammar for Week Seventeen
Founding of Western Europe, Founding of England and Ireland

1. Who was the first French king who was baptized a Catholic Christian? Clovis I

2. In what year was Clovis I crowned king? 485

3. What does the Catholic Church call France? The Church's first daughter

4. Who defeated the Muslims and stopped them from overtaking what would become France in 732? Charles Martel (Charles the Hammer)

5. Who became the first Holy Roman Emperor in 800? Charlemagne (Charles Martel's grandson)

6. What was the educational and philosophical movement Charlemagne promoted in Europe called? The Carolingian Renaissance. Charlemagne supported learning

7. After Charlemagne's son died, what happened to his empire? It split into three

8. Who and what did the Romans conquer in A.D. 43? Britain

9. When did the Roman soldiers leave Britain? 410

10. Which barbarian tribes invaded Britain? Angles, Saxons, Jutes, and later, Vikings

11. Who was the first Anglo-Saxon king? King Alfred the Great

12. When did Alfred the Great rule? In the 800s

13. Who invaded Britain and Ireland in 800s-1000s? Vikings

14. Who led the last successful invasion of England? 1066, at the Battle of Hastings, William the Conqueror

Grammar for Week Eighteen
Feudalism

1. Who settled along the rivers of Black and Baltic Seas in the early 6th century? Slavs

2. In the 800s, who conquered the Russian Slavs? Swedish Vikings

3. What were common practices of the Russians and Vikings? Human sacrifice and polygamy

4. In the ninth and tenth centuries, what did many of the Russians convert? They converted to Christianity

5. Who is known as the Apostle to the Russians? Saint Vladimir

6. Who conquered the Russians in the 1200s? Mongols

7. Who defeated the Mongols? Grand Duke Ivan and the Russians

8. Who was a very cruel Medieval Russian leader? Ivan the Terrible

9. What was the economic system of Medieval Europe? Feudalism

10. In feudalism, who was at the head? The King

11. What did the serfs do? They worked on the farms

12. What did the knights do? They protected the serfs, fought in wars, and served the king

13. What was the manor? The manor was the center of the village, where the lord and his wife lived, and it acted as the hospital.

Grammar for Week Nineteen
The Age of Faith, Medieval Art and Education

1. What provided hope, education, and medicine during the Medieval Ages? The Roman Catholic Church

2. What ended the European practice of human sacrifice and polygamy? The Roman Catholic Church

3. What can different levels of power be called? Hierarchy

4. What abuses occurred in the Church from 800s – 1000s? bribery, having children

5. What movement cleaned up the Church? The Cluniac Reforms

6. What was it called when someone spoke against a belief of the church? Heresy

7. What was a punishment for heresy? Excommunication – a person would be kicked out of the church

8. What did cardinals do? Cardinals advised the pope, and they chose the pope

9. Who supported the arts and education in Medieval Europe? The Roman Catholic Church

10. Describe Romanesque architecture: thick walls, small windows, rounded arches

11. Describe Gothic architecture: tall windows, much lighter inside

12. What was illumination? Monks would copy the Bible and literature and decorate the books

13. Who maintained literature? The Monks

14. What did ST. Thomas Aquinas teach? He taught that faith and reason go together

15. What did Father Roger Bacon help develop? The Scientific Method

Grammar for Week Twenty
The Crusades, Conflict Between Kings and Popes

1. In what year did Muslims conquer the Holy Land from the Christians? 638

2. What do Christians call the land where Jesus lived? The Holy Land

3. From 1015-1241 Christians fought to win back the Holy Land and to force the Muslims to allow Christians to pilgrimage to the Holy Land. What were these battles called? The Crusades

4. Did the Christians win any land in the Crusades? No

5. Did the Muslims lose anything in the Holy Land? The Muslims agreed to stop harassing, kidnapping, or killing Christians who go to the Holy Land on pilgrimages.

6. What is investiture? This is the power to choose the bishop.

7. Did the Pope or the King have the power of investiture? The Pope and the King fought over this power. Sometimes, the Pope held this power. Sometimes, the King held this power.

8. What are powers the Pope held over the King?

    a. Excommunication: the Pope could kick someone out of the Church, and that meant they were going to hell.

    b. Interdiction: The Pope could rule that no church services would occur, like no baptisms, no weddings, no funerals. The people would then rise up and force the king to change his policies.

9. What powers did the king have over the Pope?

    a. The army

    b. Feudalism- the king controlled the economy

Open-Ended Socratic History Question #6
Medieval Europe

Medieval Europe generally means the period of history from the fall of the Roman Empire (A.D. 476) to the beginning of the Modern Age (c. 1500). During this time, medieval Europeans developed political systems, religion, and ways of living that would lead Europe into a prominent position in the world. Two institutions, the Crown (which the king represents) and the Roman Catholic Church (which the Pope represents) battled over political power.

Answer the question "Who held more political power in the medieval ages in Europe, the Crown or the Roman Catholic Church?" Defend your answer using sound evidence.

You should be familiar with the following names and terms:

medieval monasteries	feudalism	Papacy	monarch
Charlemagne	Emperor Henry IV	Magna Carta	Islam
habeas corpus	Judaism	Crusades	interdict
excommunication	Catholic Church	St. Thomas Aquinas	

A. Monarchism in Medieval Europe
Politics

Politics is the art or science of governing or ruling. In looking at the different groups in a medieval society and comparing their political power, you can decide how important politics was in the everyday life of a medieval European. Did the political rights of a person determine how he lived, how he thought, and how he acted? Because Europe has so many countries, and because primarily the English founded the U.S.A., we will look at English monarchy in the year 1295 to fill in this graphic organizer.

Title of the Ruler of England

[   ]

Members of Parliament

[   ]

Poor Farmers Who Had No Say in Politics

[   ]

Questions:
1. What was the title of the ruler of England in 1295?_____
2. Which group(s) of English society was represented in Parliament in 1295? _____
3. In 1295, who had no political power in England?_____
4. Did the king have any power or control over the Catholic Church in 1295?_____
_____
5. Was there ever an event in English medieval ages where a king acted violently against a leader of the Catholic Church? What happened?_____
_____
_____

B. Feudalism in Medieval Europe
Economics

Economics is how a person, or society, makes, sells, and distributes commodities (stuff). Studying economics helps us understand how people bought and sold items, and how people farmed and got food on the table. While working on this page, think how important a role economics had in the daily life of a medieval person.

Leader

1.

Large, Powerful Landowners

2.		2.

Warrior Class

3.		3.		3.

Poor Farmers Who Worked the Land

4.

Questions:
1. Who was the supreme leader of the land? (In chess, his wife is very powerful.)_____
2. Who were the landlords of medieval farm property? _____
3. Who promised to fight a certain number of days a year in return for land?_____
4. Who were not allowed to move from the property they farmed and were the lowest class in medieval society? _____
5. Could somebody from the Catholic Church, such as a priest or a bishop, own land and also be a knight or a lord?

C. Power Struggles: the Crown and the Roman Catholic Church

Here are two examples of a power struggle between kings and the Catholic Church during the European Middle Ages (476–1500). Use your textbook and logical thinking to fill in the blanks.

King Henry IV (1056-1106) and Pope Gregory VII

King Henry IV and Pope Gregory VII disagreed over who should have the power to ____ bishops and priests. The king and the Pope _____ wanted the power. Because King Henry IV would not follow the Pope, Gregory VII _____ the king. English nobles and bishops would not support the King, because they were _____ of excommunication. King Henry IV traveled to the Vatican _____ during winter to show the Pope his humility. The King had to wait _____ days outside before the Pope would see him and accept his _____. The king and Pope then signed the _____ at Worms (1122), ensuring that only the _____ had the power to choose bishops and priests.

Church   choose   apology   both   excommunicated
Concordat   afraid   barefoot   three

King Henry II (1154-1189) and Archbishop Thomas Becket

English King Henry II got into an argument with _____ Tomas Becket about the **power** of the king. Becket fled England for France. When Archbishop Becket was in _____, King Henry II wanted Prince Henry crowned as king, but only Archbishop Becket had the power to do this. King _____ II had other church leaders crown Prince Henry as king. Archbishop _____ came back to England and _____ the bishops who had crowned Prince Henry. King Henry II got very _____, yelled in rage, and four of his knights went immediately to Archbishop Becket and _____ him to pieces in a cathedral. As punishment, the Pope made Henry build three monasteries and send 200 soldiers on the Crusades.

excommunicated   Archbishop   Henry   France
Becket   mad   hacked   power

> **Question:**
> 1. Did the Pope or the King have more power in medieval England? What evidence do you have that supports your answer?_____
> _____
> _____
> _____

D. Socratic Discussion and Reflection

When you share ideas with other students, your ideas may be reinforced, rejected, or slightly changed. Listening to your classmates' ideas will help you form your own judgment. After the class discussion, write the answer to the following prompt, "Who held more political power in the medieval ages in Europe, the Crown or the Roman Catholic Church?"

_____
_____
_____
_____
_____
_____
_____
_____
_____
_____
_____
_____
_____
_____
_____
_____
_____
_____
_____
_____
_____
_____
_____
_____

Grammar for Week Twenty-Two
Liberty, Muslims, and Jews

1. Which medieval country offered the most liberty in the world? England

2. What did the English king have to sign in 1215 that limited his power? The Magna Carta

3. Who was the last person to conquer England? William the Conqueror, in 1066

4. In 1289, England started the oldest representative group of people. What was this called? The Parliament

5. What documents in America show that Americans were strongly influenced by the English? The Declaration of Independence and the Constitution

6. Who controlled most of Spain and Portugal from 700 – 1492? Muslims, called Moors

7. How did Muslims treat Christians from 700 – 1000? Christians could practice their religion, but only in private.

8. How did Muslims treat Christians from 1000-1492? Christians were not allowed to have the Bible in their possession.

9. What was Reconquista? Christians of Spain retook Spain from the Muslims.

10. Where were the Jews from Spain originally from? Jerusalem. The Roman Empire kicked them out of the Holy Land.

11. By law, what profession could Jews hold in Spain? Banking

12. What were pogroms? They were massacres where Christians killed Jews.

Grammar for Week Twenty-Three
The Fall of Medieval (Feudal) Society

1. Crop Rotation: Farmers rotated which crops they grew on land in order to keep the land fertile.

2. Letters of Credit: Merchants travelled with a piece of paper that explained what the paper was worth. These letters of credit allowed merchants to travel safely without carrying gold or other valuable items.

3. Guild: Medieval tradesmen formed associations to perfect their work and to make more money.

4. Longbow: The longbow was a powerful weapon that could propel an arrow so fast and strong it would pierce armor.

5. Hundred Years' War: From 1337 to 1453, France fought England.

6. Bubonic Plague: This epidemic, also called Black Death, killed more than 1/3 of Europeans between 1347 and 1400.

Grammar for Week Twenty-Four
The Renaissance

1. The arts: The arts mean the application of human skill and imagination, particularly in visual form.

2. Philosophy: Philosophy means a way of thinking about the world and ideas.

3. Trade: A trade can refer to a craft or a business.

4. Religion: In the Renaissance, the Catholic religion was the main supporter of the arts.

5. Science: Applied science, such as the scientific method, became more important during the Renaissance.

6. Cartography: Cartography means map making. Europeans greatly expanded knowledge of the world.

7. Anatomy: Anatomy is the branch of science related to bodily structure of humans and animals.

8. Astronomy: Astronomy is science that relates to space and celestial bodies.

9. Dante: Dante was an Italian writer who authored Inferno.

10. Leonardo da Vinci: Da Vinci was a Florentine artist, sculptor, and engineer.

11. Guttenberg: Johannes Gutenburg is credited with introducing the printing press to Europeans.

12. Shakespeare: Englishman William Shakespeare is revered by many as the greatest playwright of all time.

13. Renaissance Humanism: Renaissance Humanism was a movement of artists and educators who tried to honor God by improving speech, writing, and education.

14. Michelangelo di Lodovico Buonarroti Simoni: Known as Michelangelo, this Florentine was a sculptor, painter, architect, and poet of the Renaissance.

Reading for Week Twenty-Four
The Renaissance

Beginning of the Renaissance

Renaissance means "rebirth" in French and refers to Europe from about 1300-1500. Europeans became interested in Classical Greece and Rome. They created works that glorified the individual and nature and not only religion. The Renaissance affected education, the arts, science, religion, and nearly every aspect of life in Europe. It marks the end of the Medieval world and the beginning of the Modern world. The Renaissance started in the city-state of Florence, and spread north throughout other Italian city-states and Europe.

Francesco Petrarch (1304-1374), was a Florentine lawyer and cleric who spent much time reading and writing poetry and essays. Petrarch thought that his own era – what he termed the "middle years" - offered no great examples of a good person. Instead, he admired ancient people, such as St. Augustine and Cicero, and thought that the ancients should be studied and emulated. Petrarch promoted the idea of Humanism.

Humanism in the 1300s meant classical scholarship – the ability to read, understand, analyze, and to emulate great Greeks and Romans. The Humanists were teachers of speaking and writing, called rhetoricians. They felt that by appreciating the writings of the ancient world they could learn the wisdom they needed to choose the right way in life. Humanists sought the highest virtues from the Church Fathers and also from the greatest ancient pagan authors.

Giovanni Boccaccio (1313-1375), a Florentine and friend of Petrarch, agreed with Petrarch. He focused on ordinary people in society. His novel, *The Decameron*, was a frank discussion of adult relationships, aimed at amusement. It was a sharp contrast to literature in the Medieval Ages, which focused solely on God's providence.

Florentines decided that they would promote the study of the ancients. In 1396, they invited Greek scholar Manuel Chrysoloras (c.1350-1415) from Constantinople to teach Greek at the university. At this time, Muslim Ottomans were threatening to conquer the last remnant of the once glorious Roman Empire. Over the next half century, Greek professors continued to flee Constantinople with ancient Greek and Latin manuscripts and taught at the University of Florence.

This trend spread throughout Italy: scholars studied the ancients, improved speaking and writing skills, emulated ancient art, literature, and even copied politics and social values. By the 15th century, the great works of the classical world and the Church Fathers entered the entire western world for the first time since the fall of the Western Roman Empire in 476.

Classical education in the Renaissance sometimes followed the teachings of Petrarch but not always. Works of history became increasingly analytical. However, at times education stressed memorization of classics over analysis. The classically educated person also learned proper manners. *The Courtier* by Baldassare Castiglione (1478-1529) stressed good behavior.

During the Renaissance, artists and architects emulated Classical Greek and Roman art and created incredibly beautiful sculptures, paintings, and buildings. Masters such as Leonardo de Vinci, Michelangelo, and Rafael beautified cities and homes with art that showed the glory and beauty of the human. Their work remains with us today as examples of amazing works of art.

Renaissance in the South
The Renaissance began in Florence, Italy, in about 1300 and spread to other prosperous Italian city-states that traded with the Mediterranean world. Patrons from Florence, Venice, Genoa, and Milan commissioned artists to create beautiful statues and buildings and to develop literature, science, and philosophy. The chief supporters of the arts and sciences were the nobility and the Catholic Church and artists.

Artists applied the lessons of the humanists to their art. They emphasized nature, the human figure, beauty, and perspective. Artists looked to ancient Greece and Rome for inspiration. For the first time since ancient times, nude bodies were depicted.

The "Renaissance Man" was one of many talents in the arts and literature. In the Medieval Ages, artists remained anonymous and were seen as instruments of God and the Church. In the Renaissance, artists became "rock stars."

Leonardo de Vinci (1452-1519) of Florence was a sculptor, architect, scientist, engineer, and painter. His most famous paintings are the Mona Lisa and The Last Supper. As military engineer of Florence, he designed the city's defenses. He designed plans for machineguns, airplanes, tanks, and helicopters, even though no engine existed to power these machines!

Michelangelo di Lodovico Buonarroti Simoni (1475-1564) of Florence was a painter, sculptor, architect, and poet. His two greatest patrons were Lorenzo de Medici, ruler of Florence, and Pope Julius II. He painted the Sistine Chapel in Rome, painting 10,000 square feet of Bible scenes in four years. His statues of David and the Pieta are world renown. He designed the great Dome of St. Peter's Cathedral.

Filipo Brunelleschi (1377-1436) of Florence designed a huge dome for the cathedral in Florence. It was the first dome since the Roman times.

Donatello (1386-1466) of Florence was perhaps the greatest sculptor of the 15th century. Donatello sculpted two statues, St. Mark and St. George, in a style reminiscent of Roman classicism. This was the first time in over 1,000 years that a sculptor had shown statues to have human personalities. Donatello invented the art of "schiacciato," a sculpture raised from a flat surface. He also sculpted David, the first large-scale, free-standing nude statue of the Renaissance.

Raphael (1483–1520) was a master painter and architect. He is known for painting groups of important figures, such as his paintings of the School of Athens and Disputa. His themes were from the classical world and the religious world. He became the chief architect of St. Peter's Cathedral. With Michelangelo and Leonardo de Vinci, he is known as being one of top three Renaissance painters.

Writers of the Renaissance wrote in the vernacular, not in Latin. Writing reflected common earthly themes, instead of religious ones. Giovanni Boccaccio (1313-1375) of Florence wrote *The Decameron*, a frank discussion of adult themes. Unlike Medieval literature, it was meant for recreation. Niccolò Machiavelli (1460-1527) of Florence wrote *The Prince,* a book how a strong ruler should seize and hold power. From Machiavelli we received the teaching, "The ends justifies the means." This means that a strong ruler should, or does, whatever it takes to get his goal. Dante Alighieri (1265-1321) of Florence wrote *The Divine Comedy* in Italian. Before this, all major works were written in Latin. It is a book detailing Dante's journey through hell, purgatory, and into heaven. Dante encounters hundreds of people along the way. Vasari (1511-1574) wrote the first book on the history of art, detailing the most influential artists of the Italian Renaissance. To this day, his book is used to understand Western painting.

Renaissance in the North
The Renaissance, the rebirth of classical thought and art that began in Florence, spread throughout Europe in the 14th and 17th centuries. In the North, the Renaissance is known for an invention, paintings, literature, and music.

Perhaps the most important invention of the Renaissance was the Gutenburg Press by German Johannes Gutenburg (c.1400-1468). Before this, writers copied literature by hand, a painfully slow process. Gutenberg invented movable type which used metal letters that could be arranged and rearranged to form words. A machine called a press held the letters in place while a paper was pressed over it. Gutenburg's method sped up the process of copying literature and was so effective it remained the main printing method for 400 years. The first book that was printed with this method was the Gutenburg Bible, made c. 1455. The Gutenburg Press enabled the ideas of the Renaissance to spread quickly throughout Europe.

Oil painting developed in the north, in Netherlands. Flemish painter Jan Van Eyck (1390-1441) perfected this art. Van Eyck produced a new look to painting that created paintings that were vivid in detail. He discovered that by boiling a solution of mixed piled glass, calcined bones (bones burned to ashes) and mineral pigments in linseed oil, he could create a painting that was vibrant in color and light. He kept this knowledge secret until a few years before his death. Albrecht Durer (1471-1528) is regarded as the best German artist of the Renaissance. He painted altarpieces, portraits and self-portraits, and copper engravings. He is perhaps the first entrepreneurial artist. Declining to work solely for the nobility or church, he sold his paintings with his wife on the market. The paintings of Dutch Rembrandt van Rijn (1606-1669) could be the most recognizable of Northern European Renaissance artists. Rembrandt used vivid color and light and shadows. His paintings were of biblical and historical figures, and also featured ordinary people in portraits.

Writers during the Renaissance broke from tradition by writing in the vernacular instead of Latin, making fun of tradition and religion, attacking superstition, ridiculing medieval notions of chivalry, and focusing on individuals. Englishman Geoffrey Chaucer (1340-1400) wrote *The Canterbury Tales*, the story of a pilgrimage to the tomb of St. Tomas Becket at Canterbury. In his story, pilgrims tell stories that highlight the lives of individuals in humorous ways. Dutch writer Desiderius Erasmus (1466-1536) attacked superstition and ignorance. Erasmus favored a reform of the Church but was against its division. He wrote a Greek translation of the New Testament, and essays on theology, education, and philosophy. Englishman William Shakespeare (1564-1616) was perhaps the greatest playwright of all time. He wrote of famous characters in history, such as *Julius Caesar* and *Henry V,* and he wrote of intriguing stories of love, murder, and humor in *Hamlet* and *Romeo and Juliet*. In Spain, Miguel de Cervantes (1547-1616) wrote *Don Quixote*, a story of an older man who believes he is a middle-aged knight who must fight for noble causes. His servant is Sancho Panza. De Cervantes ridiculed romantic ideas, but at the same time, honored them.

The center of Renaissance music was in the Low Countries of Northern Europe (Belgium, Luxembourg, the Netherlands). In the 14th and 15th centuries, musician Johannes Ockeghem, Dufay, and Josquin des Prez composed music that was no longer reliant on vocals. Instrumental music became dominant.

The Renaissance in the north changed society in many ways. The Gutenburg Press allowed ideas to spread quickly. Artists created new methods to make vivid paintings, and writers penned comedic and moving plays and novels.

Open-Ended Socratic History Question #7

The Renaissance

In the early medieval ages up to the fourteenth century (1300), European civilization lagged behind Asian and Middle Eastern cultures in areas such as medicine, science, and trade. However, this was soon to change. From A.D. 1300 to 1700, Europeans greatly changed many aspects of their lives. Amazing advances were made in the arts, cartography, trade, technology, and science. This time period is known as the Renaissance, which is a French word for "rebirth." It describes a rebirth of interest in classical arts, classical literature, and a great desire to discover.

Answer the question "During the time of the Renaissance in Europe (A.D. 1300-1700), what three aspects of life changed the most?"

the arts	philosophy	trade	religion	science
mathematics	cartography	anatomy	astronomy	Dante
da Vinci	Guttenberg	Shakespeare	exploration	humanism
Silk Road	Michelangelo			

A. Change over Time

Change over time refers to the idea that people, countries, groups, knowledge, and just about everything changes during a period of time. As students of history, we should be aware of changes, and we should be able to analyze and see how these changes affect people. Just think how much the invention of the car changed how people travel! Or, imagine a life where our society would still have slavery. To understand change in societies is important as a historian.

For this exercise, list the term you researched and write very briefly how it changed from 1300 to 1700. Then rate how big of a change this was on a scale of 1 to 10, 10 being the biggest change. The first two are done for you. (Of course, don't include the names of people!)

Term	Change	Rate
1.	1.	1.
2.	2.	2.
3.	3.	3.
4.	4.	4.
5.	5.	5.
6.	6.	6.
7.	7.	7.
8.	8.	8.
9.	9.	9.
10.	10.	10.

B. Socratic Discussion and Reflection

When you share ideas with other students, your ideas may be reinforced, rejected, or slightly changed. Listening to your classmates' ideas will help you form your own judgment. After the class discussion, write the answer to the following prompt, "During the time of the Renaissance in Europe (A.D. 1300-1700), what three aspects of life changed the most?"

_____
_____
_____
_____
_____
_____
_____
_____
_____
_____
_____
_____
_____
_____
_____
_____
_____
_____
_____
_____
_____
_____
_____

Grammar for Week Twenty-Five
The Reformation

1. Ninety-five theses: It is believed Martin Luther nailed a document with 95 complaints against the Catholic Church on the door of a church.

2. Salvation: Salvation means deliverance from sin and entry into heaven.

3. Indulgences: An indulgence means the remission of punishment for sin.

4. Excommunication: Excommunication means when the Catholic Church kicks someone out of the Church.

5. Act of Supremacy: King Henry VIII made himself King of England and this Act forced all English to swear loyalty to him as leader of the English Church or be executed.

6. Tudor: King Henry VIII was a member of the Tudor family.

7. Protestant: A Protestant is a Christian who was/is not a Catholic.

8. Church of England: The Church of England is a Protestant Christian Church founded by King Henry VIII.

9. Counter-Reformation: The Counter-Reformation is also called the Catholic Reformation and means when the Catholic Church changed policies and practices.

10. Predestination: Many Protestant Christians believed in predestination, the idea that at birth God already determined who was going to heaven.

Reading for Week Twenty-Five
The Reformation

Causes of the Reformation

European society underwent great changes from 1300-1600. Religious reformers led a movement to change the Catholic Church and to found new Christian religions. Catholics and those who left the Church, called Protestants, fought religious wars that redrew the political map of Europe.

Many Europeans grew skeptical of the Pope, the leader of the Christian Church, in part because of corruption and disorder. At one time, there were three popes, called the Great Schism of the West (1378-1417). One of the Popes lived in Avignon, France, while the others were in Rome. Some clergy (priests) were corrupt and sought financial gain. They sold church offices (simony) or rewarded relatives with important positions (nepotism). Others sold dispensations to raise money. A dispensation allowed a group to forego close adherence to a church rule. Some priests had wives and children, even though they promised to not have relations with women.

Misuse of funds from indulgences angered reformers. An indulgence is a release from temporal punishment due to a sin committed. Medieval Christians believed that when one sinned, they needed to seek forgiveness from God and they needed to seek purification from the causes of their sin. Purification could happen either on Earth or in purgatory, a cleansing area between earth and heaven. An indulgence released a Christian from temporal punishment. By sacrificing something of value with a repentant heart, a Christian could gain an indulgence. An indulgence could be gained through taking a pilgrimage, or by praying. The Medieval Church encouraged individuals to purchase indulgences, and priests were to send the money to Rome to help build St. Peter's Cathedral. Some priests kept the money and sold indulgences without caring if the sinner was repentant.

Reformers agitated against the Church's teachings on salvation. From its beginning, the Catholic Church had two traditions of salvation teaching. St. Augustine and other Church Fathers had written that salvation came from loving God and having faith in him. However, the Church also stressed participation in rituals and receiving the blessings of the sacraments led to salvation. Many Europeans yearned for a more personal God. In Spain, the Church allowed for a more personal faith, but not elsewhere.

Englishman John Wycliffe (1320-1384) taught at Oxford University against the supreme authority of the Church and promoted believers to have a stronger reliance on the Bible. He challenged the idea of transubstantiation, the idea that during mass a priest turns a wafer of bread and wine into the body and blood of Jesus. He believed in predestination, the idea that only the elect were chosen to be saved. The Church removed Wycliffe from Oxford.

Jan Hus (1369-1415) of Bohemia was a priest and president of Charles University in Prague. During this time, at the mass the priests could receive both bread and wine, but the laity could receive only the bread. Hus taught and practiced that all should share in the host and wine, not just the priests. The Church promised him safety if he were to explain his ideas. However, the Church tried him in the city of Constance, found him to be a heretic and had him burned at the stake. Led by Jan Zizka, "Hussites" revolted and beat the Holy Roman Empire in war. They founded a new church, called "Utraquist Church" where all could receive wafer and wine.

In the Late Middle Ages, the power of the merchants and the king grew at the expense of the princes. Princes resented sending tax money to Rome to empower the Catholic Church. They were interested in how they could gain independence from the Pope and from the Holy Roman Emperor. The Reformation eventually allowed many princes to break from the Pope and the Holy Roman Empire, and these princes no longer had to send tax money to the Church.

The Reformation and Martin Luther
Martin Luther (1483-1546) is the central figure of the Reformation. A German monk, Luther initially protested against the Church by reportedly nailing a list of grievances on a church door in Wittengurg. Known as the "Ninety-five Theses," Luther protested the wrongful sale of indulgences, the Church's teachings on salvation, the authority and corruption of the Church, celibacy of the priests, and taught the need for a more personal relationship with God. Luther was an Augustinian Friar who had great troubles coming to terms with man's sinful nature. He had trouble completing his first mass, because he felt he wasn't worthy to preside over transubstantiation. He became to believe that God could not look on man's efforts with kindliness, and that only Jesus' acts were necessary for salvation.

Where Luther lived, Church leaders competed for pilgrims to flock to their towns to donate and spend money. Duke Frederick of Saxony collected relics to attract pilgrims. Brother Johann Tetzel peddled indulgences seemingly only to collect money. Repulsed at these abuses, Luther chose to start a new Church. He publicly called for a rebellion against the Church, and wrote that the Pope was the Antichrist.

In 1520, Pope Leo X excommunicated Martin Luther. Holy Roman Emperor Charles V. summoned Luther to explain himself at the Diet (Congress) of Worms. Luther marched on Worms a hero, proclaiming he would not recant against his conscience. For one year, Duke Frederick III of Saxony protected Luther at the Wartburg Castle. Luther wrote three books that became the cornerstone of Protestantism. He taught:
    1. faith alone suffices for salvation
    2. the Bible alone was the only guide to Christianity
    3. Christians could interpret the Bible on their own.
Luther established a new religion, known as the Lutheran Church. It was very similar to the old Catholic religion. However, Luther denied the presence of Jesus in the Eucharist and rejected celibacy. He married a former nun and had six children.

In 1534, Luther translated the Bible into German and continued his religious revolution. The printing press allowed the Bible, and his writings, to be widely disbursed. In his writings, he attacked certain parts of the Bible, such as Epistle of St. James, calling it the "Epistle of Straw." This part of the Bible explains that faith without works is dead. At the Diet of Speyer in 1529, German princes protested the Diet's decree that no religious innovations be allowed. From then on, all who accepted religious reform were known as Protestants. Followers of the traditional Church were known as Roman Catholic.

German Peasants believed that the break from the Church also meant that nobles should relinquish their greater privileges and revolted. The princes and Luther disagreed. With Luther's support, the princes crushed the Peasant Rebellion and killed over 100,000.

After, a civil war in Germany broke out between the Holy Roman Emperor who sided with the Catholic Church and many German princes who sided with Luther. It ended with the Peace of Augsburg (1555). It was decided that whichever religion the prince was, the people in his area would adopt that religion, as well.

As head of a new religion, Luther had great influence on European affairs. His teachings seemed to encourage people to be more self-reliant, less eager to follow authorities, and less likely to be monarchists. Luther also made controversial decisions. He granted a dispensation to Prince Phillip I of Hesse and allowed him to take a second wife. He strongly opposed dissent by the peasants in the crushing of the Peasant Rebellion.

Spread of the Reformation
The Reformation spread throughout Europe in the sixteenth century. Most known of the Protestant leaders were Ulrich Zwingli in Zurich, John Calvin in Basel, and King Henry VIII of England. Some radical reformers tried to alter society but were crushed. The Reformation was not about religious freedom. Wherever Protestantism spread, leaders set up a theocracy where no dissension was tolerated.

Ulrich Zwingli (1484-1531) of Zurich, Switzerland was a priest and humanist. He broke from the Catholic Church, rejected celibacy and the sacraments, and taught the importance of correct behavior. Zwingli established a tribunal with informers to ensure all acted correctly. Zwingli banished all rituals and outlawed any practice of Catholicism. He brought back the practice of public confession of sin.

Some protestant reformers were violently crushed both by the Catholics and other Protestants. The Anabaptists believed that people should be baptized as adults. In Munster, Germany, Melchiorites established a society that practiced polygamy, abolished private property, and made their city into a fortress. Protestants and Catholics crushed Anabaptists and the Melchiorites.

John Calvin (1509-1564) was the second major Protestant figure after Luther. A layman in France, he fled to Basel, Switzerland after writing against the Catholic Church. In

Basel, he wrote the "Institutes of the Christian Religion", a thoroughly-detailed apology of Protestantism. Calvin taught that Scripture alone was the authority for the Christian, and he believed in predestination. Like Luther, he thought that man's free will was limited. Calvin also taught that God predetermined who was saved, the elect, and who was damned. Calvin rejected all sacraments (Luther had accepted Eucharist and Baptism). He destroyed all icons, such as crucifixes, statues, sacred paintings, vestments, altars, confessionals, and stained-glass windows depicting saints.

Although Calvin taught predestination, he believed people were obligated to act in ways to make God happy. To enforce this, he established a very strict theocracy in Geneva, Switzerland, outlawing all other religions. There was no dancing, card playing, drinking, or braiding hair. Each home was inspected twice a year by religious police. The Censor had to initial each page of a new book. The opposition was tortured and burned at the stake.

Throughout Europe, Calvin's ideas inspired the formation of other Protestant religions. In Holland it was Dutch Reformed Church. In Scotland, John Knox formed the Presbyterian Church. French Calvinists were called Huguenots. English Calvinists were called Puritans. Many Huguenots and Puritans brought their hard work ethic and strict moral code to America.

In England, King Henry VIII (1509-1547) was unable to have a son with his Spanish wife Catherine. He unsuccessfully petitioned the Pope for an annulment. (An annulment is like a divorce, except the Church declares that there was no marriage to begin with.) King Henry VIII broke from the Catholic Church and remarried, eventually marrying six times. (He beheaded two of his wives!) In 1534, the English Parliament issued the Act of Supremacy that made Henry the leader of the new Church of England. Anyone who would not follow Henry and stayed with the Catholic Church risked his life.

A period of religious struggle ensued in England. King Henry VIII closed all monasteries, seized church land, and banned all Catholic practices. Hundreds were beheaded and many were hung, drawn, and quartered because they would not swear an oath to the King. After his Protestant son Edward VI's short rule, his daughter Mary I (1516-1568) tried to bring Catholicism back by force during her five years of rule. Trying and executing hundreds who would not convert back to Catholicism, she was given the name "Bloody Mary." After her rule, Henry's Protestant daughter Elizabeth I (1533-1603) ruled for almost 45 years. Elizabeth I successfully planted Protestantism in England. She banned all public Catholic practices, executed over a hundred Catholics, and imprisoned thousands to enforce the Act of Supremacy.

The Catholic Revival or The Counter-Reformation
During the time of the Reformation, the Catholic Church implemented reforms to purify the Church. Catholic historians call this movement the Catholic Reformation, emphasizing it was wholly Catholic. Protestant historians call this movement the

Counter-Reformation, implying that it happened purely as a result of the Protestant Reformation. Evidence for both sides exist.

In the first half of the sixteenth century, the Catholic Church lost millions of European faithful to various Protestant Churches. Among the countries that remained Catholic, kings asserted a great deal of autonomy. The French king could choose the bishops and the Spanish set up their own Inquisition. The Catholic Church was hurt by its practices of simony, nepotism, wrongful sale of indulgences, and its failure to express clearly its doctrine of salvation. Still, many more Europeans remained Catholic than converted to Protestantism. Familiarity, history of helping the poor, help with overcoming sin, the sacraments, and the biblical foundation of the early Christian Church were strong reasons to remain Catholic.

The election of Pope Paul III (served 1534-1549) changed the course of Catholic history. He crusaded against Church abuses, appointed learned and able Cardinals, and called for the Council of Trent (1545-1563). The council was a meeting of world Catholic leaders that clarified Church teachings and renewed Catholic spiritualism.

The Council taught that Scripture and Church are the two authorities for Christian life. Luther had taught that Scripture alone was needed. The Council asserted that the human will is completely free and that salvation is from faith and actions. Luther had taught that man's will was limited because of his sinful nature, and that a person could not fully participate in his own salvation because of his fallen grace. Calvin had taught that man's salvation was predetermined and that he could do nothing for his own salvation. Luther had denied the human action of the writing of the Scripture. The Catholic Church stated that normal men were inspired by God to write the Scripture, and that God used their faculties to do so. The Council argued that all seven sacraments are channels of real grace, that Christ is present in the transubstantiation, and that priests and ceremonies are important. Ritual was stressed, and gorgeous decorations of churches were promoted.

The Catholic Church founded a Roman Inquisition to fight Protestantism and created an "Index of Forbidden Books," which outlawed the reading of heretical works. It forbade the sale of indulgences and improved the education of local priests.

In the sixteenth century, mysticism flourished in the Catholic Church. Mystics seek the Holy Trinity in a personal way, in prayer, without a priest. Teresa of Avila (1515-1582) is the most well-known female Catholic mystic. She established the Order of the Carmelite Reform, a contemplative order of nuns with convents throughout Spain. Ignatius Loyola (1491-1556) is the most well-known male Catholic mystic. He founded the Society of Jesus, also called the Jesuits. He was injured fighting as a knight in the Crusades. Recovering, he imagined the outline of a book he later wrote called the "Spiritual Exercises." The book deals with the discipline and training needed for a faithful life. Ignatius believed people had free will and were not wholly dependent on the actions of God for their salvation.

The Jesuits four areas of concentration were 1. Preaching, 2. Hearing confessions, 3. Teaching, 4. Missionary Work. They reorganized Europe's universities and opposed execution of heretics. Ignatius of Loyola made great demands on his followers, and they were successful in converting tens of thousands in Asia and the Americas.

Open-Ended Socratic History Question #8
The Reformation

Since the time Christians believe Jesus Christ walked the earth (c. A.D. 4) for over 1500 years there had been one major organized Christian church in Western Europe, the Roman Catholic Church. In sixteenth - century Europe, however, many Christians were upset with the Roman Catholic Church for reasons of faith, corruption, and personal gain. Some Christians tried to change the Church from within, but others formed new religions. The Christian churches that formed were known as "Protestant" because believers were "protesting" the Catholic Church.

Two major Protestant reformers were Martin Luther and King Henry VIII. These men found so much support against the Catholic Church that they founded new religions, the Lutheran Church and the Anglican Church. Compare and contrast the reasons Martin Luther and King Henry VIII had in founding new religions.

Be familiar with these terms and people in your essay:

Ninety-five theses	salvation	divorce	indulgences
Excommunication	Act of Supremacy	Tudor	Protestant
Church of England	Counter-Reformation	corruption	

A. Compare and Contrast

To **compare** means to look at two or more objects and recognize what they have in common. To **contrast** means to look at two or more objects and recognize what they have different from each other.

For this assignment, fill in the chart below to help you compare and contrast. Under "Martin Luther" and "King Henry VIII," write how the two men differed in their conflicts with the Roman Catholic Church. Under "Similarities," write what the men had in common in their protest against the Church.

Martin Luther		King Henry VIII
Differences	**Similarities**	**Differences**

B. Socratic Discussion and Reflection

When you share ideas with other students, your ideas may be reinforced, rejected, or slightly changed. Listening to your classmates' ideas will help you form your own judgment. After the class discussion, write the answer to the following prompt, "Compare and contrast the reasons Martin Luther and King Henry VIII had in founding new religions."

_____
_____
_____
_____
_____
_____
_____
_____
_____
_____
_____

Grammar for Week Twenty-Six
The Scientific Revolution

1. Scientific Revolution: In the Scientific Revolution, man looked to observation instead of ancient writings or religion for answers about the natural world.

2. Scientific Method: In the Scientific Method, experimentation and observation became the method of knowledge.

3. Nicolaus Copernicus: Copernicus (1473-1543) argued that the sun was the center of the universe. He used mathematics to posit his theory.

4. Galileo Galilei: Galileo (1564-1642) invented the telescope and proved the sun was the center of the universe.

5. Isaac Newton: Newton (1643-1727) put forth the theory of gravity and laws of motion. Many regard him as the most influential scientist of all time.

6. Francis Bacon: Bacon (1561-1626) developed the scientific method.

7. Renee Descartes: Descartes placed the human at the center of all.

8. Andreas Vesalius: Vesalius examined dead humans and detailed human body correctly.

9. William Harvey: Harvey explained how the circulatory system works.

10. John Locke: John Locke wrote that government should mainly protect life, liberty, and property

Reading for Week Twenty-Six
The Scientific Revolution

In the 15th, 16th, and 17th centuries, Europeans changed the way they studied science. Scientists such as Rene Descartes, Sir Francis Bacon, and Galilei Galileo developed the use of the scientific method, a system of study that is aimed at reaching verifiable conclusions. A number of inventions during this time enabled scientists to make breakthroughs in the fields of astronomy, medicine, physics, chemistry, and navigation. Historians call this the Scientific Revolution.

The scientific method is a process scientists use to find natural explanations. These explanations help humans find solutions to diseases, enabled man to understand how the sun is the center of the universe, and can be used to make human life last longer.

Step one in the scientific method is to understand the problem. The scientist then makes a hypothesis, or guess, to explain it. The hypothesis is tested with an experiment that can be repeated. If the hypothesis does not resolve the problem, the scientist creates a new hypothesis and tests this with an experiment.

If the hypothesis solves the problem, other scientists test the hypothesis. If the same results are reached, the hypothesis is accepted as a theory. A theory becomes a law if it is applicable universally.

New inventions like the telescope and the microscope enabled scientists to test theories of the natural world. The telescope is used to gaze at stars. It was invented in the Netherlands by eyeglass makers Hans Lippershey and Hans Janssen in the early 1600s. Galileo made great improvements of it and used it to formulate his heliocentric view of the world. Lippershey and Janssen also developed one of the first microscopes, used to investigate small objects. Galileo made improvements to their invention, as well.

The thermometer and barometer were developed during this time. Galileo was one of the scientists who worked on both of these, as well. The thermometer is used to measure the temperature of water or air, and the body. The barometer is used to measure the atmosphere by using water, air, or mercury and can predict short term weather.

Throughout the Medieval Ages, ancient Greeks dominated medicine. Hippocrates (460-377 B.C.) observed the human body and was a noted doctor. Aristotle (384-322 B.C.) wrote about the function of the parts of the body. Galen (A.D. 129-199) made observations of animals, performed experiments, and explained the parts of mammals.

Scientists of the Renaissance greatly improved medicine by use of the scientific method. Belgian Andreas Vesalius (1514-1564) was the first to dissect dead humans. He published a book on human anatomy, *On the Fabric of the Human Body*. He is the founder of modern human anatomy. Englishman William Harvey (1578-1657) explained the circulatory system in his book, *On the Motion of the Heart and Blood*. Before his

work, it was thought blood flowed to and from the heart through the same vessels via a tidal system. Irish Robert Boyle (1627-1691) started modern chemistry.
Before the Scientific Revolution, humans had relied on deductive reasoning as a way to resolve medical issues. After, inductive reasoning became the primary method of coming to scientific knowledge. Aristotle had used logic to come to general principles. With these general principles, he wrote how he thought the world should operate. The scientific method, however, requires huge amounts of data. Analysis of this data creates theories, or laws, on how the natural and physical world operates.

For over 1,000 years, Europeans had relied on ancient Greek writings, the Catholic Church, and the Bible to explain how the natural world operated. Church Fathers and the Greek Aristotle, Ptolemy, and Galen dominated the fields of religion, philosophy, education, physics, astronomy, and medicine. In the 15th, 16th, and 17th centuries, all of this changed

At the end of the Renaissance, Europeans altered how they thought about and studied science so much that we call this period the Scientific Revolution. Instead of relying on the Church or Greek writings, all scientific ideas were put to the test of observation and experimentation. Whatever was no quantitative, such as religious experience, was increasingly viewed with a skeptical eye.

Frenchman Rene Descartes (1596-1690) was a mathematician who questioned the ability to have knowledge with absolute certainty. He wrote in *Discourse on Method* "I think, therefore I am", and posited that the only thing a person can know is his own existence. He was skeptical of any knowledge that dealt with the outside world, unless it could be verified by data.

Englishman Sir Francis Bacon (1561-1626) furthered this idea of relying on provable data to understand the world. In *Novum organum*, published in 1620, Bacon wrote that reason would help man form a more comfortable and better civilization. Through observation of much data, man could form general theories. Aristotle had written that man take general logical theories to explain the world.

Astronomy led the way in the Scientific Revolution. Polish priest and astronomer Nicolaus Copernicus (1473-1543) observed the orbit of the planets. Using mathematical calculations, he refuted Ptolemy's understanding that the sun revolved around the earth. In *On the Revolutions of the Heavenly Bodies* he argued that the sun was the center of the universe.

Through observation and experimentation, two other scientists strengthened Copernicus' arguments. Danish astronomer Tycho Brahe (1576-1601) observed that the planets orbited in an elliptical, not circular, orbit. His assistant German Johannes Kepler (1571-1630) illustrated with a mathematical formula that Copernicus was correct.

Galilei Galileo (1564-1642) of Italy went beyond previous scientists by using observation and experimentation to prove verifiable conclusions. Until Galileo, scientists had argued their findings were theories. Using a telescope he improved from a Dutch lens crafter, Galileo confirmed Copernicus' theories about a heliocentric world.

Galileo came into conflict with Catholic Church authorities. His *Dialogue on the Two Chief Systems of the World* (1632), showed that only a simpleton could believe in a geocentric world. He wrote that the Bible supported his findings. The Church supported a geocentric viewpoint of the world and forbade most from interpreting Scripture. It wanted Galileo to say his conclusions were theories. He refused. Galileo was placed under house arrest but was allowed to continue his work.

Englishman Sir Isaac Newton (1642-1727) brought together the theories of Copernicus and Kepler and the observations of Galileo to formulate laws governing falling bodies. In *Mathematical Principles of Natural Philosophy*, published in 1687, he presented three laws to describe how the universe worked:
    1. Motion continues in a straight line without force,
    2. The rate of change of motion is determined by the forces acting on it, and
    3. Action and reaction between two bodies are equal and opposite.
Newton rejected Descartes's view that the mind and reason could understand the world and believed it possible to prove everything he said by mathematics or experiment.

Open-Ended Socratic History Question #9
The Scientific Revolution

For over 1400 years, the western mind had accepted writings of ancient Greek, Roman, and religious writers to explain not only religious thought but science and nature as well. Then, within the next 200 years, a radical change took place. Instead of accepting ancient writings on science and nature without question, western philosophers and scientists strove to experiment and observe what really exists. The results of this change in thought and action were incredible. We call this change "The Scientific Revolution." The Scientific Revolution affected how the western mind thought, believed, and acted.

Answer the question "Which three changes in thought or action were the most important in the Scientific Revolution, from 1500–1800?" Describe the Scientific Revolution and identify the most important individuals and breakthroughs in this time period. Your answers may be a specific discovery, an invention, an idea/theory, or anything else that is relevant.

Be familiar with these terms in your essay:

Scientific Revolution	scientific method	Copernicus	Galileo
Kepler	Newton	telescope	thermometer
barometer	Bacon	Descartes	John Locke
Andreas Vesalius	William Harvey		

A. Rate the Change

List the terms you have researched, and briefly describe the change. Then rate the importance of this change with "1" meaning the most important change, "10" meaning the least important change.

Term /Person	Description of Change	Rating
1.	1.	1.
2.	2.	2.
3.	3.	3.
4.	4.	4.
5.	5.	5.
6.	6.	6.
7.	7.	7.
8.	8.	8.
9.	9.	9.
10.	10.	10.

Question: Which three changes do you rate as the greatest?

B. Socratic Discussion and Reflection

When you share ideas with other students, your ideas may be reinforced, rejected, or slightly changed. Listening to your classmates' ideas will help you form your own judgment. After the class discussion, write the answer to the following prompt, "Which three changes in thought or action were the most important in the Scientific Revolution, from 1500–1800?"

_____
_____
_____
_____
_____
_____
_____
_____
_____
_____
_____
_____
_____
_____
_____
_____
_____
_____
_____
_____
_____
_____
_____
_____

Grammar for Week Twenty-Seven
The Age of Exploration

1. Trade in the Renaissance: Italian city-states traded with Byzantine and Arab traders

2. Caravel: This ship was durable, travelled well against the wind, was big enough to carry much supplies, and made open-ocean travelling possible.

3. Prince Henry the Navigator: This Portuguese nobleman sponsored sailors to explore the world.

4. Bartholomeu Dias: This explorer was the first to sail around the Cape of Good Hope.

5. Vasco de Gama: This explorer was the first to sail from Europe to India.

6. Christopher Columbus: This sailor discovered America in 1492 for Spain.

7. The Treaty of Tordesillas: The Catholic Church brokered this treaty that split the New World between the Spanish and the Portuguese.

8. Balboa: This sailor was the first to sail the Pacific Ocean.

9. Magellan: This sailor led an expedition that went around the world.

10. Americus Vespucci: This Italian was the first to write that Columbus had discovered a new continent. America is named after him.

Reading for Week Twenty-Seven
The Age of Exploration

During the Renaissance (1300-1500), Italian city-states such as Florence, Venice, and Milan grew incredibly wealthy. Italian sailors traded with the Byzantine and Arab traders. Traders would then sell Asian products throughout Europe. Problems with this arrangement led Europeans to seek better trade routes.

To get the Asian silks, spices, and jewels, Atlantic coast Europeans had to pay middle men higher fees for products. In 1453, the Muslim Ottoman Empire conquered Byzantium and monopolized the land trade east. At times, Muslims would harass the traders, killing or enslaving the crew and taking the ships. Atlantic coast Europeans wanted an alternate trading route with Asia.

The Spanish believed they had a duty to spread the Catholic religion to the world. In 1492, the Spanish had just finished fighting a 700 year war against the Muslims who had conquered Spain in the early medieval ages.

What made long sea travel possible technologically? A durable ship that travelled well against the wind called the caravel was introduced. Use of the compass and astrolabe improved navigation and allowed sailors to navigate on the open sea, away from sight of land.

The Portuguese led the way in exploring the world. Small, rocky, and inhospitable for agriculture, Portugal had relied on its sailing for survival throughout history. Prince Henry the Navigator had successfully fought the Muslims in Cueta in North Africa in 1415. He built a home overlooking the ocean and founded a school to train sailors to sail east, around Africta, and into India.

Prince Henry's dream was realized after his death when Bartholomeu Dias sailed around the tip of Africa in 1488. Dias named the tip the "Cape of Storms". The king renamed it "Cape of Good Hope." Portuguese Vasco de Gama reached India and returned with jewels and spices in 1498. Portugal had its all-water route east to Asia.

Christopher Columbus (1453-1506) of Genoa was a sailor with a dream. After studying a map by Toscanelli', he thought he could reach India by going west from Europe 3,500 miles. King Ferdinand V and Queen Isabella I of Spain accepted his plan and supported him with three ships: the Nina, the Pinta, and the Santa Maria.

After 33 days of travel where his crew nearly mutinied because they feared for their lives, Columbus found land. He thought he was in India and called the natives Indians. He actually landed on an island in the Caribbean. Spain thought it had a water route west to Asia.

To avoid conflicting claims of new lands, Portugal and Spain signed The Treaty of Tordesillas (1494) that split the world in two. An imaginary line of demarcation was drawn: Portugal received everything east of the line, and west of it got Spain.

The legacy of Columbus is one of achievement and cruelty. Europeans settled the new land and brought with them Christianity, literacy, and western law and customs, but native peoples were often brutalized and died from new diseases.

The Spanish continued to explore. Vasco Nunez de Balboa discovered the Isthmus and the Pacific Ocean in 1513. Magellan's voyage around the world proved the existence of North and South America.

Working as an observer, Americus Vespucci wrote Spain had discovered a new continent. A German scholar read his ideas and drew a new world map, naming the new continents America.

The search for an all water route west to Asia (now called the Northwest Passage) continued. Italian John Cabot explored Canada and New Foundland for England in 1497 and 1498. Frenchman Jacques Cartier (1534 and 1541) explored St. Lawrence River and eastern Canada.

Open-Ended Socratic History Question #10
The Age of Exploration

From the 1400s through the 1600s, European countries embarked on amazing journeys of exploration and discovery throughout the world. Known as "The Age of Exploration," Portugal and Spain led Europe in discovering the Americas, opening up Asia further for trade, and paving the way for colonization of the New World.

Answer the question "What were the two most important causes of the Age of Exploration?" In your answer, list and briefly describe the great voyages of exploration. Also, research these terms to help determine your answer:

Renaissance	spices	Asia	Italy	Dias
Vasco de Gama	Columbus	Magellan	Cabot	Jamestown
Portugal	Spain	France	England	Holland
Enlightenment	Prince Henry the Navigator			

B. Cause and Effect

Cause and effect is a term that means one event made another event happen. For example, if you push against the pedals of your bicycle, the bicycle moves. In this example, the push against the pedals is the cause and the bicycle moving is the effect.

CAUSE --------------------------------→EFFECT
push against pedals---------------→bicycle moves

In social studies, cause and effect usually relates events and people. The relationship is trickier to understand than the above example with the bicycle. Sometimes it is difficult to see causes and effects in history.

Write down the cause on the left. In the middle, write the effect of each cause. Then rank the most important causes of the Age of Exploration 1 to 10 with 1 being the most important.

Term (Cause)	Effect	Rank
1.	1.	1.
2.	2.	2.
3.	3.	3.
4.	4.	4.
5.	5.	5.
6.	6.	6.
7.	7.	7.
8.	8.	8.
9.	9.	9.
10.	10.	10.

Copyright ©2019 by The Classical Historian. All Rights Reserved

C. Socratic Discussion and Reflection

When you share ideas with other students, your ideas may be reinforced, rejected, or slightly changed. Listening to your classmates' ideas will help you form your own judgment. After the class discussion, write the answer to the following prompt, "What were the two most important causes of the Age of Exploration?"

_____
_____
_____
_____
_____
_____
_____
_____
_____
_____
_____
_____
_____
_____
_____
_____
_____
_____
_____
_____
_____
_____
_____
_____

Grammar for Week Twenty-Eight
Geography and Great Civilizations of Mesoamerica and South America

1. Mesoamerica: This word is from Greek and means "middle America." It is an are in central America.

2. Maya: This civilization existed from c. 1500 B.C. to A.D. 1697 in Mesoamerica.

3. Slash and Burn Agriculture: Mayas used to burn trees and use the ash as fertilizer for their farms.

4. Inca Empire: This empire was located in the Andes Mountains and lasted from c. 1200 – 1672.

5. Inti: This was the sun god of the Incas.

6. Aztecs: The Aztecs established an empire in the area of modern-day Mexico City from c. 1100 – 1521.

7. Hernando Cortes: This Spaniard conquered the Aztecs and the Mayans.

8. Francisco Pizarro: This Spaniard conquered the Incas.

Grammar for Week Twenty-Nine
The Mayas and The Incas

1. Yucatan Peninsula: The Mayas settled primarily in the Yucatan Peninsula.

2. Maya Society: Maya society was split into three groups: the nobles, the commoners, and slaves.

3. Maya Sacrifices: Mayas sacrificed prisoners of war, slaves, and even children to appease their gods.

4. Maya sport: Mayas played a team ball game involving a hoop.

5. Maya Calendar: Mayas used an accurate solar calendar.

6. Maya Glyphs: Mayas used ideographs for writing.

7. Conquistadores: Spanish soldiers conquered the Mayas and ended the Maya Empire in 1697.

8. Mayas: This tribe ruled an empire from c. 1500 B.C. to 1697.

9. Aztecs: This tribe, also known as the Mexica, established an empire from c. 1200 to 1520 in the area that is present-day Mexico City and the area around it.

10. Chinampas: Aztecs built rectangular floating gardens to grow crops in the waters around their capital city.

11. Tenochtitlan: This was the capital city of the Aztecs.

12. Human Sacrifice: Aztecs sacrificed humans to their sun and war god on a monumental scale.

13. Montezuma II: He was the last Aztec emperor.

14. Hernan Cortes: The Spaniard Cortes conquered the Aztecs in 1520.

Grammar for Week Thirty
Incas and Northeast

1. Incas: This tribe built an empire that stretched along the western coast of South America from c. 1200 to 1572.

2. Inti: This was the Incan sun god.

3. Incan "golden rules": Do not steal. Do not lie. Do not be lazy.

4. Cuzco: This was the Incan capital city.

5. Machu Picchu: This was an estate built for an Incan emperor.

6. Francisco Pizarro: This Spaniard conquered the Incas.

7. Hunting and Gathering: The Northeast Native Americans subsisted mainly through these two activities.

8. Iroquois: Europeans called the Northeast American Indians this name.

9. Longhouse: The Iroquois lived in these wooden buildings, sharing it with many families.

10. Sachems: Women chose 50 men to be leaders of the Iroquois nations.

11. Polygamy: This word means the practice of one man having many wives. The Iroquois Indians did this.

12. Great Spirit: Most American Indians believed that one spirit ruled all of nature's spirits.

Grammar for Week Thirty-One
Southeast, Plains, Great Basin, and Plateau Indians

1. Economy of the Southeast Indians: These Indians were mainly farmers.

2. Chickees: These homes of Southeast Indians were made of logs with a roof covered in leaves or grasses.

3. Plains Indians: These Indians depended on buffalo for meat, clothing, homes, and on buffalo dung for fires.

4. The horse: The Spanish brought this animal to America in the 1500s and 1600s.

5. Tipi: This house of the Plains Indians was easy to move and was made of buffalo hide and wooden poles.

6. Great Basin Indians: These nomadic Indians were hunters and gatherers and used baskets for storage.

7. Plateau Tribes: These tribes were named after the Columbian River plateau.

8. Shaman: This man was believed to be able to talk to or receive information from supernatural spirits. He was also the tribe's medicine man.

Grammar for Week Thirty-Two
The Southwest, California, Northwest Coastal, Subarctic, and Arctic Tribes

1. Pueblos: This is the name Spanish explorers gave to all Indians living in what is now the Southwestern United States.

2. Economy of Pueblo Indians: They were farmers and hunters and gatherers.

3. Taos Pueblo: In this city, some Indians live in buildings that have been inhabited for over 1,000 years.

4. Economy of Northwest Coastal Indians: They fished salmon, hunted seals and whales, and gathered shellfish.

5. Potlach: This was a ceremonial party in which the host gave away gifts to the guests.

6. Kayak: This boat used by the Inupiat is a skin covered canoe.

7. Igloos: This is a home of the Inupiat built out of ice blocks.